English 1B

Lina

Tim

Ian

Alice

Duckie

Judy Ling • Anne Smith

Marshall Cavendish
Education

Summary of Contents

Vocabulary	Speaking	Writing	Listening/Phonics	Hands On!
Rooms and things in a house	• Asking politely • Expressing thanks	Using prepositions to write about things in a house	• Identifying prepositions of position • Beginning sounds 'j', 'k' and 'r'	Asking politely and role-playing
Places in a neighbourhood	Asking and telling where one lives	Writing addresses	• Identifying types of housing and places in a neighbourhood • Beginning sounds 'w' and 'y'	Writing about my neighbourhood
Things in a supermarket	Asking for assistance	Using countable and uncountable nouns	• Identifying items in a supermarket • Beginning sounds 's' and 'z'	Writing a shopping list and role-playing
Things in a garden	Using 'Do you/they', 'Does he/she/it' to ask questions	Using 'this', 'that', 'these' and 'those'	• Identifying items in a garden • Beginning sounds 'q' and 'x'	Drawing and describing things in my garden
• Farm animals and their young • Verbs related to animals	Talking about animal sounds	Using full stops, question marks and commas	• Listening to simple instructions • Beginning sounds hard 'c' and soft 'c'	Choosing animals for my farm

6 Let's Help Out!

I help you
And you help me.
That is what makes
A family.

Help your friends
And neighbours too.
You help them
And they will help you.

Do you help your family, friends and neighbours? How do you help them?

Your Turn!

Read the questions. Circle the correct answers.

1. Who helps  ?

   A.   B.   C.

2. Do you help your family? Yes / No

3. Who shares with  ?

   A.   B.   C.

4. Do you share things with your friends? Yes / No
   What do you share? Tell your friend.

I am Amy. Everyone helps out in my family.
Sometimes, Sam and I offer to help.

Mum cooks dinner.

Grandma waters the plants.

Sometimes, others help us.

Please take us to the park, Dad.

Dad takes us to the park.

Grandpa reads us a story.

Thank you, Grandpa.

Your Turn!

Role-play Amy and her family. Remember to say **please** and **thank you**. Here are some ideas:
- Amy and Sam ask Dad to help them build a toy.
- Dad asks Sam to bring him the newspaper.

Sam and I help out around the house.

I help Dad in the **living room**.

Sam helps Grandpa and Grandma in the **bedroom**.

We help Mum in the **kitchen**.

Your Turn!

Draw and name one other thing that you can find in your living room, bedroom and kitchen.

Living room	Bedroom	Kitchen

_____   _____   _____

Sam and I want to help Mum look after our baby sister, Alice. But where is she?

Is she **on** the sofa?
No.

Is she **behind** the door?
No.

Is she **in** the cupboard?
No.

Is she **beside** the television?
No.

Is she **under** the bed?
Yes.

We like to look after Alice.

Your Turn!

Help Dad find his glasses. Complete the questions.

1.   Are they _____?

2. Are they _____?

3.   Are _____?

4. _____?

Two Men and a Fish

Tom and Nick go fishing.

"I have a fish!" cries Tom.

Tom pulls at his fishing line.
But Tom cannot bring the fish in.
It is too heavy.

"Can I help you?" Nick says.

Nick helps Tom bring the fish in.
What a big fish!

"Thank you for helping me," Tom says.
"We can share the fish."

Who catches the fish? How does Tom thank Nick for helping him?

What do you think would happen if Nick did not help Tom?

Listen and Do!

Listen to what Amy and Mum say.
Tick (✔) the correct box.

Let's Listen!

Listen to the poem.
Listen out for the beginning j sound.

Jilly said,
"I do like jelly.
I think jelly
Is quite jolly."

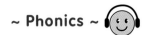

Listen to the poem.
Listen out for the beginning k sound.

The **k**eeper gave the **k**ey
To the **k**angaroo,
And it let all the animals
Out of the zoo.

Listen to the poem.
Listen out for the beginning r sound.

It's **r**aining on the **r**ooftops
And everything I see,
But I have my **r**aincoat on,
It cannot get me!

Worksheet 8, page 10

I CAN!

Tick (✔) the boxes to show what you can do.

☐ I can offer help by asking **Can I help you?**

☐ I can say **please** and **thank you**.

☐ I can name things at home.

☐ I can say where things are by using **on**, **behind**, **in**, **beside** and **under**.

NEW WORDS

living room	sofa	television	telephone
kitchen	plate	fork	spoon
cup	bowl	bedroom	bed
cupboard	lamp	_____	
_____	_____	_____	

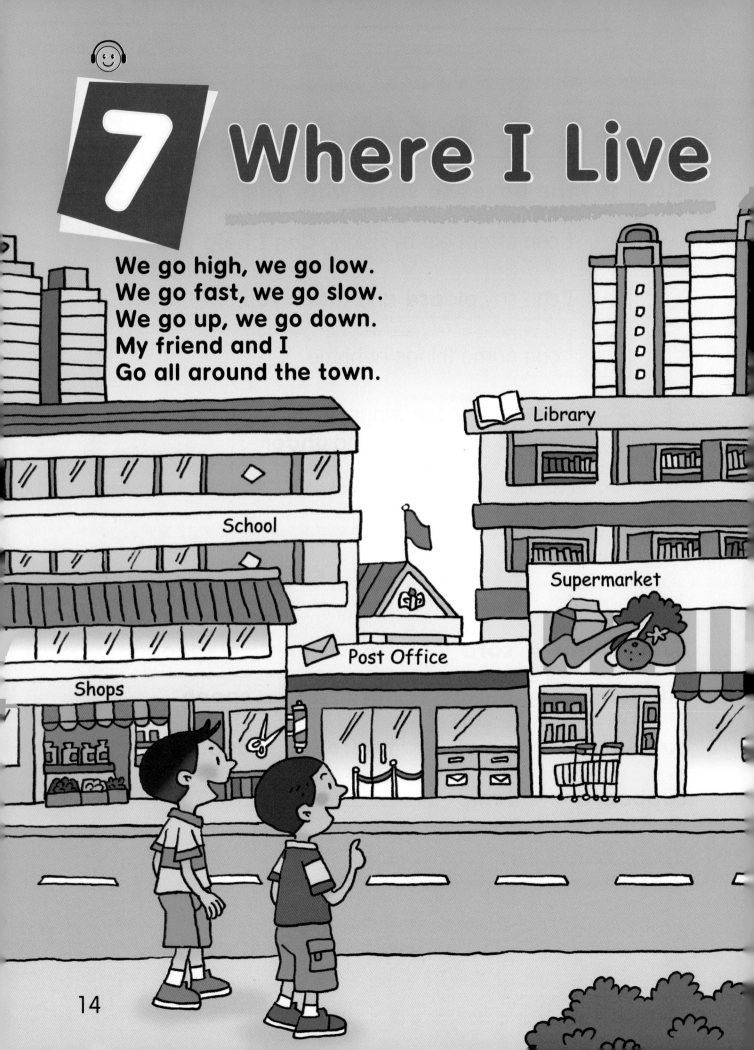

7 Where I Live

We go high, we go low.
We go fast, we go slow.
We go up, we go down.
My friend and I
Go all around the town.

Library

School

Supermarket

Post Office

Shops

14

Your Turn!

Read the questions. Complete the answers.

1.   Where do the boy and his friend go?

They go all around the t_____.

2.   What do they see?

They see some shops,

a s_____,

a p_____ _____,

a s_____m_____

and a l_____.

What can you see
in your town?

John lives in a house. **He** likes **his** house.
It has a big garden.

John visits **his** friend, Alice.
Alice lives in a flat. **She** likes **her** flat.
Her flat has big windows.

We use **he**, **she**, **they**, **we** and **you** to talk about people.

Leo and Daisy visit John and Alice. **They** live in a different neighbourhood. **Their** neighbourhood is very big.

neighbourhood

Welcome to **our** neighbourhood. **We** are glad that you are here!

How about **you**? Tell me about **your** home.

The words **my**, **your**, **his**, **her**, **our** and **their** show who or what something belongs to.

Your Turn!

On a sheet of paper, draw a picture of your home.
Tell your friend about your home.
Example: This is **my** _____.

Show and tell the class about your friend's home.
Example: This is **his / her** _____.

The children go for a walk in their neighbourhood.

The children are at the shopping centre.

Your Turn!

What is there in your neighbourhood?
Tell your friend.
Examples: There is a **supermarket**.
There are many **shops**.

The children go to the post office.
Daisy posts a letter.
Look at the address on the letter.

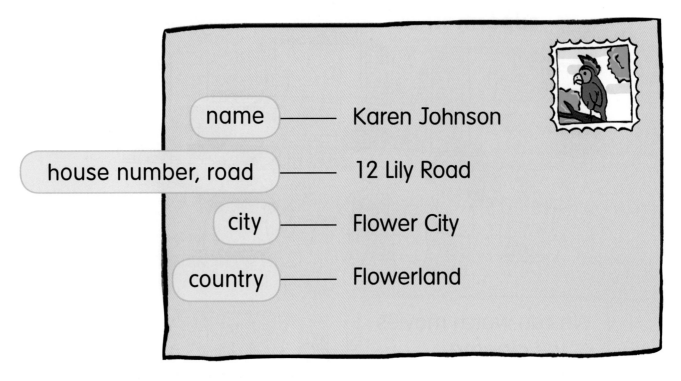

name ——— Karen Johnson

house number, road ——— 12 Lily Road

city ——— Flower City

country ——— Flowerland

Your Turn!

Write your name and address below.

My name is _____.

I live at _____

_____

_____

_____

_____

The children ask each other where they live.

Your Turn!

Ask your friend where he/she lives.
Tell your friend where you live.
Example: **Where do you live?**
        I live at _____.

Grandpa's House

One night, we go to Grandpa's house.

We see a frog sleeping behind the door.
We see two birds sleeping beside the window.
We see three hens sleeping on the sofa.
We see four rabbits sleeping under the bed.
We see five cats sleeping on the bed.

"Where do you sleep, Grandpa?" we ask.

"In the garden," says Grandpa.

How many animals are there in Grandpa's house?

Why does Grandpa sleep in the garden?

Listen and Do!

Listen to the sentences.
Tick (✔) the correct boxes.

1.

2.

3.

Let's Listen!

Listen to the poem.
Listen out for the beginning **w** sound.

A **w**alrus in a **w**aistcoat
Would be a funny sight.
A **w**alrus in a **w**aistcoat
Would give you quite a fright.

Listen to the poem.
Listen out for the beginning **y** sound.

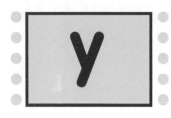

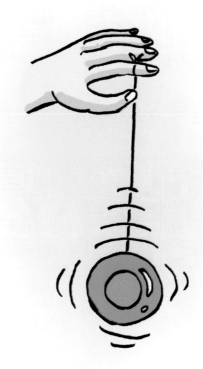

Can **y**ou make
Your **y**o-**y**o go
Up and down
And high and low?

I CAN!

Tick (✔) the boxes to show what you can do.

☐ I can use **my**, **your**, **his**, **her**, **our** and **their**.

☐ I can name the places in my neighbourhood.

☐ I can write my address.

☐ I can say where I live.

NEW WORDS

house   flat   shops   library

neighbourhood   supermarket   cinema

police station   fast food restaurant

post office   _____   _____

_____   _____   _____

8 Let's Go Shopping

Do you go shopping with your family? What does your family buy?

Mum shops. Dad shops.
You shop. I shop.
We shop in the morning.
We shop at night.
We shop when it is dark.
We shop when it is light.
Why do you think it is
That people just can't
Stop shopping?

Your Turn!

Look at the picture on page 26.
Circle the people who shop.

Read the poem. Answer the question.

When do the people shop?

They shop in the _____ and at _____.

Susan and her father are at the supermarket.
They go to the fruit section.

Your Turn!

Which fruits do you like? Tell your friend.
Example: I like bananas.

There are many things at the supermarket.

Your Turn!

What else can you find in a supermarket? Share your answer with your partner and make a class list.

Susan looks at her shopping list.
What do they need to buy?

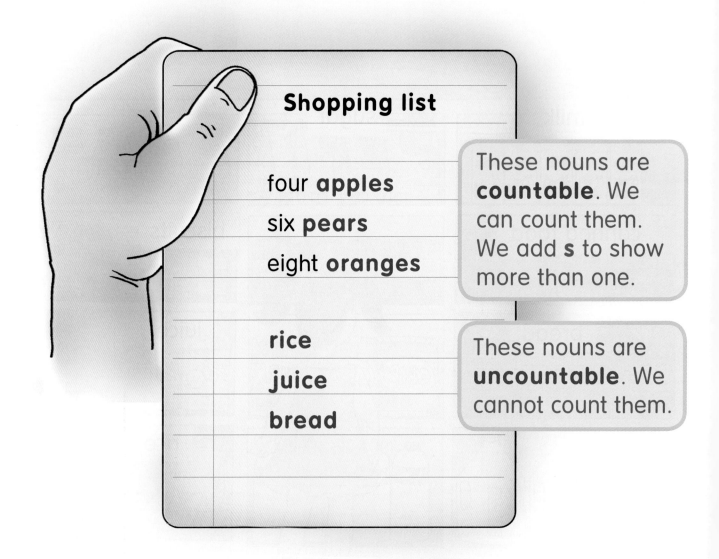

Shopping list

four **apples**

six **pears**

eight **oranges**

rice

juice

bread

These nouns are **countable**. We can count them. We add **s** to show more than one.

These nouns are **uncountable**. We cannot count them.

Your Turn!

**Can you think of more nouns that are uncountable?
Tell your friend.**

Your Turn!

Match and write the items in the correct list.

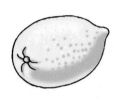

Countable nouns	Uncountable nouns
_____	_____
_____	_____
_____	_____

At the meat section, a woman is buying a chicken.

Your Turn!

Role-play Susan and a shop assistant. Buy the things on the shopping list on page 30. Use the phrases on this page.

Worksheet 5, page 26   33

Shopping with Mum

Mum gets some peas. We do not like peas.

She gets some potatoes. "Yuck!" we say.

She gets a chicken. We do not like chicken.

She gets some milk. "Let's go home, Mum!
We don't like the supermarket," we say.

Mum gets some jelly and
ice-cream. "Yum! Yum!
Yum!" we shout.

"We love the supermarket!
And we love you, Mum!"

What do the children
like in the supermarket?
What do they not like?

What do you like in
the supermarket?

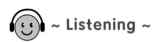

Listen and Do!

Listen to the sentences. Match the people with what they want to buy.

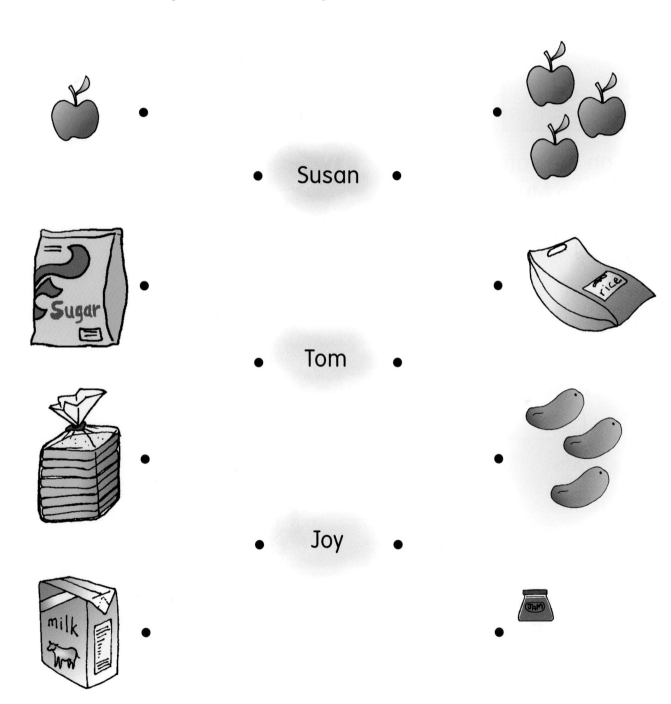

Let's Listen!

Listen to the poem.
Listen out for the beginning **s** sound.

Sit on the **s**ofa,
Or **s**it on Mum's knee,
Sit on anything
But not on me!

Listen to the poem.
Listen out for the beginning **z** sound.

Have you seen the **z**ebras
That live in the **z**oo?
If you have seen the **z**ebras,
Have they seen you?

I CAN!

Tick (✔) the boxes to show what you can do.

☐ I can name some things in a supermarket.

☐ I can name some countable and uncountable nouns.

☐ I can ask for help at a supermarket.

☐ I can thank others for their help.

NEW WORDS

bananas	papayas	oranges	plums
limes	pears	apples	lemons
grapes	milk	sugar	jam
biscuits	bread	juice	canned food
oil	rice	_____	

_____ _____ _____

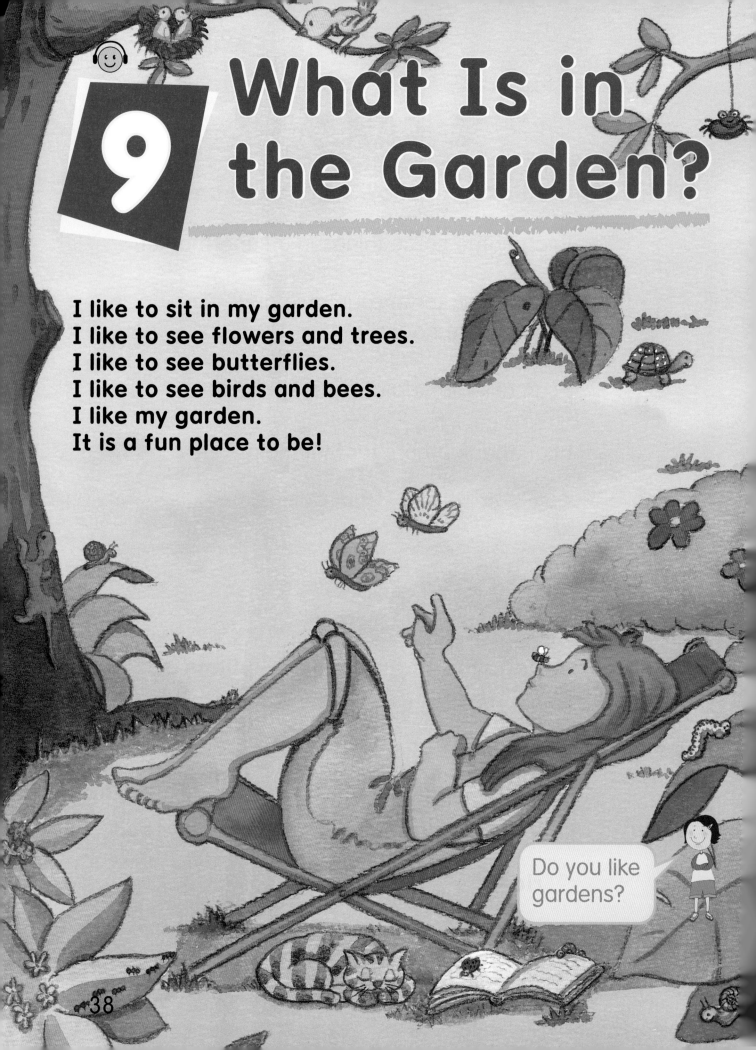

9 What Is in the Garden?

I like to sit in my garden.
I like to see flowers and trees.
I like to see butterflies.
I like to see birds and bees.
I like my garden.
It is a fun place to be!

Do you like gardens?

Your Turn!

Read the question. Complete the answers.

What does the girl like to see in her garden?

She likes to see flowers and t_____,

b_____, b_____ and

b_____.

**If you have a garden, what do you like to see in it?
Tick (✔) the boxes.**

Many plants and animals live in this garden.
Chirpy the bird lives in the garden too.

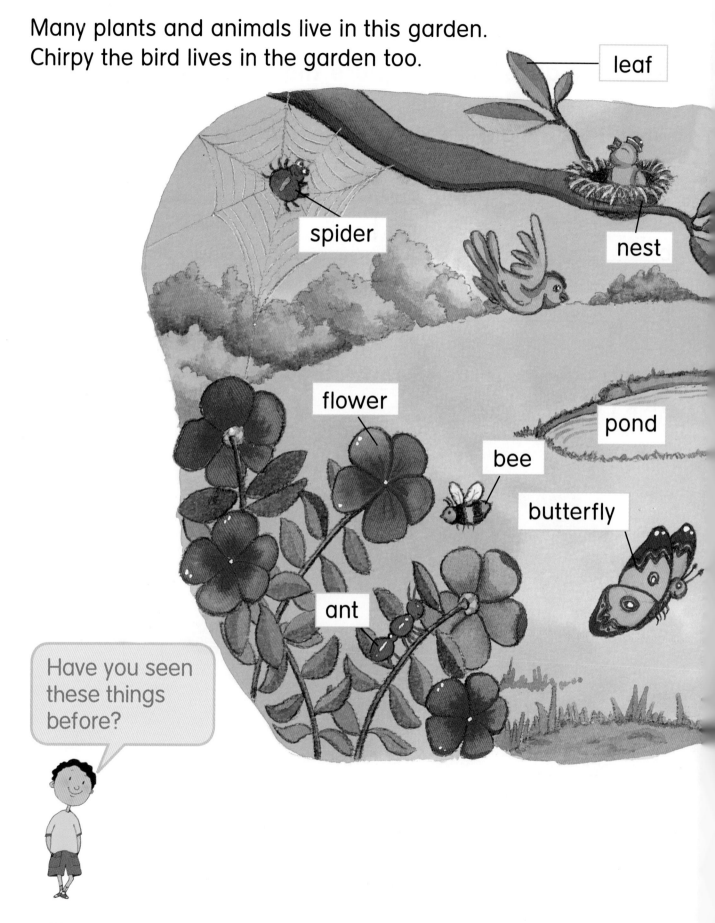

leaf

spider

nest

flower

pond

bee

butterfly

ant

Have you seen these things before?

Chirpy has a baby bird. Its name is Cheepy.
Can you find Chirpy and Cheepy?

tree

grass

snail

plant

worm

Your Turn!

Tell your friend what is in the garden near
your home or school.
Example: There are **birds**.

Chirpy takes baby Cheepy for a walk.
They see many things in the garden.
Some are near them, some are far away.

We use **this** and **these** to point to things that are near us.
We use **that** and **those** to point to things that are not near us.

Your Turn!

Use this, that, these and those to talk about things in the classroom with your friend.

Your Turn!

Look at the pictures. Then, complete the sentences.

1. _____ are bees.

2. _____ is a butterfly.

3. _____ bird.

4. _____

Cheepy asks Chirpy some questions.

Your Turn!

Look at pages 42-43. Role-play Cheepy and Chirpy.
Ask questions about the things in the pictures.
Examples: **Does it** like the garden?
Do they like flowers?

The Big, Fat Mango

In the garden, up in a tree, is a big, fat mango.

A boy is under the tree.
"I love mangoes," he says. "That is my mango."

A girl is under the tree too.
"I love mangoes," she says. "That is my mango."

Along comes a goat.
"Look at that yummy mango," it says.
"That is my mango."

They all wait under the tree for
the mango to drop. They wait
and wait.

Then, along comes a bird.
"This is my mango,"
it says. And it eats up
the mango.

Who waits for the
mango to drop?

Who eats
the mango?

Listen and Do!

Listen to the sentence. Circle the things that Chirpy sees in the garden.

Chirpy sees ...

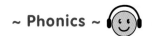

Let's Listen!

Listen to the poem.
Listen out for the beginning **q** sound.

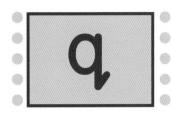

I'm sewing a quilt,
A quilt for a queen,
The prettiest quilt
You have ever seen.

Listen to the poem.
Listen out for the beginning **x** sound.

Xavier has a xylophone,
Xavier has a drum.
Xavier makes
Far too much noise,
Says his mum.

I CAN!

Tick (✔) the boxes to show what you can do.

☐ I can name things in a garden.

☐ I can use **this** and **these** to point to things that are near me.

☐ I can use **that** and **those** to point to things that are not near me.

☐ I can ask questions using **Do** or **Does**.

NEW WORDS

spider	nest	leaf	tree
flower	bee	butterfly	pond
grass	ant	snail	plant
worm	_____		_____

_____   _____   _____

10 On the Farm

Farmer Brown
has on his farm:
one cat,
two mice,
three cocks,
four hens, five chicks,
six cows, seven geese,
eight ducks, nine sheep,
ten lambs, and hidden away
where nobody sees,
a hundred and one honeybees.

(Adapted from the poem 'Farmer Jackson's Farm', by Clive Samson)

What animals are there on the farm? Have you ever been on a farm?

Your Turn!

How many of these animals are there in the picture?
Write your answers in the boxes.

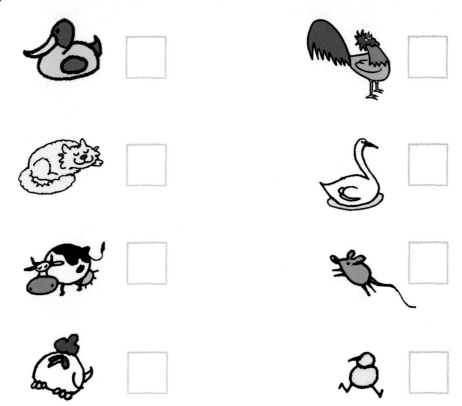

It is early in the morning on the farm.
How many young animals can you see?

There are many animals on the farm.

chick

chicks

lamb

lambs

We often add **s** to nouns to mean more than one.

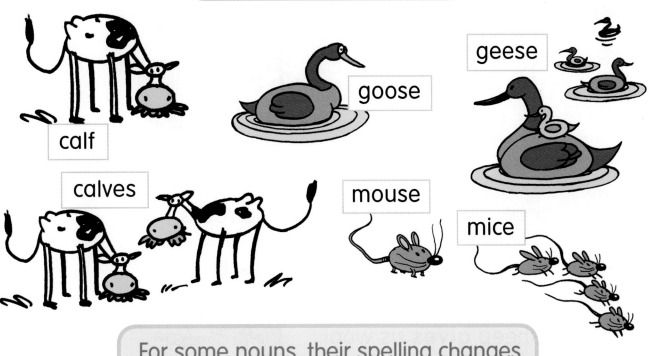

calf

calves

goose

geese

mouse

mice

For some nouns, their spelling changes when they mean more than one.

Your Turn!

Draw and name your favourite farm animal.

The animals on the farm are busy all day long.

The duck **swims** in the pond.

The hen **lays** eggs.

The cow **chews** grass.

The cow **gives** us milk.

The goat **climbs** the rocks.

The sheep **gives** us wool.

Your Turn!

How do animals help us? Tell your friend about three animals which help us.
Example: A duck lays eggs.

The animals make a lot of noise.

QUACK

The duck **quacks**.

BAAA

The lamb **bleats**.

CLUCK! CLUCK!

The hen **clucks**.

COCK-A-DOODLE-DOO!

The cock **crows**.

MOOOOOO

The cow **moos**.

MEOOOOW

The cat **meows**.

NEIGH!

The horse **neighs**.

Your Turn!

In pairs, take turns to make the animal sounds on this page. Ask your friend to guess what animal you are and what sound you are making.
Example: You are a lamb. A lamb bleats.

It is market day.
What does Farmer Brown sell?
Farmer Brown sells two hens, three ducks,
a goose and a sheep.

What does Mrs Green sell?
Mrs Green sells two geese, four hens,
a cow and two goats.

A sentence ends with a full stop (.).
A question ends with a question mark (?).
(,) is a comma. We use it to separate words in a list.

Your Turn!

John asks Farmer White some questions about his farm. Fill in the boxes with a full stop (.), a question mark (?) or a comma (,).

1. John: What do you have on your farm ☐

   White: I have chicks ☐ lambs ☐ geese and calves ☐

2. John: What do your chicks do ☐

   White: They look for worms ☐

3. John: What do your lambs do ☐

   White: They play in the field ☐

4. John: What do your geese do ☐

   White: They swim in the pond ☐

5. John: What do your calves do ☐

   White: They drink milk ☐

Do you have a question for Farmer White? Write it here.

_____

_____

Alex at the Farm

When Alex goes to the farm,
he chases the ducks.
"Quack! Quack! Quack!" they go.

He chases the cows.
"Moo! Moo! Moo!" they go.

He chases the sheep.
"Baa! Baa! Baa!" they go.

Then, the old turkey chases Alex.
It chases him up and down the hills.
It chases him all around the farm.

"Gobble! Gobble! Gobble!"
goes the turkey.

"Help! Help! Help!" goes Alex.

How do you think the
animals feel when they see
the turkey chasing Alex?

What animals does
Alex chase?

Worksheets 7 & 8, pages 48-49

Listen and Do!

How many animals are there on the farm? Listen to the sentences. Circle the correct number of animals.

1.

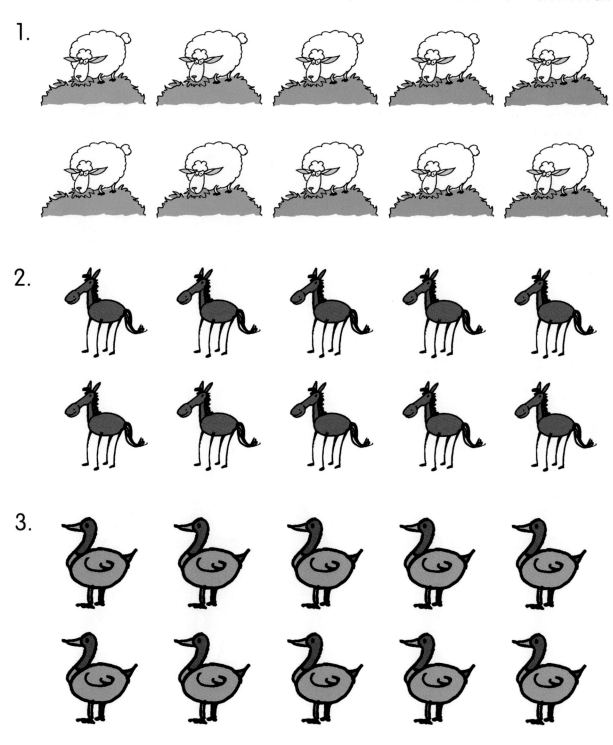

2.

3.

Let's Listen!

Listen to the poem.
Listen out for the beginning hard c sound.

We **c**an **c**omb our hair.
We **c**an wash our faces.
We **c**an brush our teeth
And we **c**an tie our laces.

Listen to the poem.
Listen out for the beginning soft c sound.

There is a **c**ircus in the **c**ity,
In a great big tent,
But what do I do
When I do not have a **c**ent?

Worksheet 9, page 50

I CAN!

Tick (✔) the boxes to show what you can do.

☐ I can name farm animals and their young.

☐ I can say what animals do.

☐ I can make some noises that animals make.

☐ I can use full stops (.), question marks (?), and commas (,) in my sentences.

NEW WORDS

hen	chick	cow	calf
sheep	lamb	duck	duckling
cat	kitten	swims	lays
chews	gives	climbs	_____

_____ _____ _____

Words I Know

Rooms in a house
living room
bedroom
kitchen

Things in a house
sofa
television
telephone
bed
lamp
cupboard
plate
fork
spoon
cup
bowl

Types of homes
house
flat

Places in the neighbourhood
neighbourhood
shops
library
police station
post office
supermarket
cinema
fast food restaurant

Names of fruit
bananas
papayas
oranges
plums
limes
pears
apples
lemons
grapes

Things in a supermarket

milk

sugar

jam

canned food

biscuits

bread

juice

oil

rice

Animals in a garden

spider

bee

butterfly

ant

snail

worm

Things in a garden

nest

leaf

tree

flower

pond

grass

plant

Animals on a farm

hen

cow

sheep

duck

cat

Young animals on a farm

chick

calf

lamb

duckling

kitten

Verbs related to animals

swims

lays

chews

gives

climbs

The words **on**, **behind**, **in**, **beside** and **under** tell us where people and things are.

The rabbit is **on** the table.
The cat is **behind** the sofa.
The bird is **beside** the cupboard.

The words **my**, **your**, **his**, **her**, **our** and **their** show who or what something belongs to.

This is **my** flat.
Jane likes **her** house.
John and James go to **their** park.

Some nouns are countable. We add an **s** to them to show more than one.

There are five banana**s** on the shelf.
May I have three orange**s**, please?

Some nouns are uncountable. We cannot count them.

There is some **rice** on the table.
I like to eat **bread**.

We use **this** and **these** to point to things that are near us.

This is a pen.
These are pencils.

We use **that and those** to point to things that are not near us.
Look over there. **That** is a flower.
Those are apples in the box over there.

We add **s** to some nouns to mean more than one.
There are three duck**s** in the pond.
Farmer Green has four cow**s**.

Some nouns change spelling when they mean more than one.
There is a mouse behind the chair and five **mice** under the table.
Farmer White has one goose and Farmer Black has six **geese**.

We use a full stop (.) to end a sentence.
Farmer Green has two horses**.**

We use a question mark (?) to end a question.
What does Farmer Brown have**?**

We use a comma (,) to separate words in a list.
Farmer Brown has one goose**,** two hens and three cats.

What I Have Learnt

How do you offer to help?
Can I help you, Dad?

How do you ask for help politely?
Please read me a story.

How do you thank someone?
Thank you.

How do you ask where someone lives?
Where do you live?
I live at 10 Daisy Road, Flower City, Flowerland.

How do you ask for assistance in a shop?
Excuse me.
May I have a mango, **please**?
Thank you very much.

How do you ask questions to find out whether someone likes something?
Does he like apples?
Do they like flowers?

How do you talk about the sound an animal makes?
The duck **quacks**.
The cow **moos**.

Notes

Hands On!

Look at the pictures. Write what the children say. Remember to use the phrases on pages 4-5. Then, act out the scenes.

1. Amy offers to help Mum.

Yes, you can.

2. Dad builds a toy for Sam.

Your toy will be ready soon, Sam.

Hands On!

What can you find in your neighbourhood?

Write sentences about your neighbourhood.

1. There is a _____.

2. There are _____.

3. There _____.

4. _____

Hands On!

Pretend you are going to have a party. What do you need to buy? Write a shopping list.

Shopping list

_____

_____

_____

_____

_____

_____

_____

Pair up with a friend.
Role-play and buy the things in your shopping list.
Remember to use the phrases on pages 32-33.

Hands On!

What do you like to see in your garden?
Draw your garden here.

What is in your garden? Tell your friends.
Examples: This is a flower.
**   Those are birds.**

Hands On!

Pretend you are a farmer. You need to buy some animals for your farm. Circle the animals you want to buy.

Write about your animals. What do your animals do?

I want to buy ___hens,_____.

The ___hens give me eggs._____

The _____.

_____

_____